G000269381

Publisher:
Bruno Alfieri
Technical consultant:
Walter Beltrami
Editors:
Ippolito Alfieri, Silvia Giacobone
Photos:
Roberto Carrer, Gabriela Noris, Guy Mangiamele
Graphic design:
Giordano Barazzetti
Production:
Massimo Fabbri, Attilio Chiozza
Translation:
Warren McManus

INDEX

ISBN 88-85880-53-3 CL 41-0240-1

La Collection®
© 1992 by Automobilia Srl
Società per la Storia e l'Immagine dell'Automobile
I-20125 Milano, via Ponte Seveso 25
All rights are reserved for all countries

PRINTED AND BOUND IN ITALY
by Grafiche Editoriali Padane, Cremona, March 1992.

BUGATTI EB 110

Stefano Pasini

AUTOMOBILIA

THE FAMILY TREE

Few marques in the world can boast the prestige of the red oval gracing the radiators of Bugatti automobiles. Perhaps no other carmaker has succeeded in creating the sort of mystique that permeates every page in the history of this "Marque des Marques" like an inebriating perfume. This alone would justify the flood of interest surrounding its resurrection.

Ettore Arco Isidoro Bugatti was born in Milan on 15 September 1881, of a family replete with artistic talent. He, too, wanted to become a sculptor but took the path of mechanical engineering instead, when he realized that his brother Rembrandt was better than he.

Throughout his life, this genial, strong-willed, often arrogant, ever formidable individual was tormented by an unbearable dread of being second best. Automobile racing must have appeared a natural choice to him for demonstrating his capabilities, when he founded his own automobile factory, after accumulating experience as an employee with Deutz, Prin-etti e Stucchi, Mathis and De Dietrich between 1898 and 1909. Success did not come overnight, however, and the cylindrical or "tank-profile" body designs of his early 8-cylinder Grand Prix creations were rather ugly. But in 1922, at the French Grand Prix, he unveiled the Bugatti Type 35, still recognized today as one of the handsomest cars ever built. It instantly began winning race after race and was followed by many other cars of equal power and performance, the racing models 37, 54, 51 and 59. Then came the Grand Sport models, like the brutal 43 or the sophisticated 55, the multi-use chassis for external bodywork (the 57 in the normal version, the lowered S version, the supercharged C version and the combination SC), the stately 41, better known as the Royale, and so forth. Those were years in which pure genius had no need of massive R&D efforts to express itself: while it is surprising that at the turn of the century Ferdinand Porsche had already constructed an electric car with four-wheel drive and steering, it is equally

Opposite page. The 1951 101, bodywork by Gangloff. It was built after Ettore Bugatti's death, using materials and components which had survived the Second World War. Above. Ettore Bugatti.

Ground plan of the Bugatti estate in Molsheim. 1. The house. 2. Museum. 3. Stables. 4. Factory gatehouse. 5. General workshop. 6. Chassis and engine assembly shop. 7. Foundry, forge and press shops. 8. Artisan workrooms. 9. Wood storeroom. 10. Spare parts despatch warehouse. 11. Turning and precision grinding shop. 12. Machine repair and maintenance. 13. Hydroelectric generating station. 14. Railcar assembly hangar. 15. Surface treatments. 16. Spares store. 17. Raw materials warehouse. 18. Annexe. 19. Analytical and research laboratory. 20. Offices. 21. Works canteen. 22. Hostellerie du Pur Sang. Château St. Jean. 24. Stables. 25. Executives' married quarters. 26. Test bench. 27. Kitchens and store.

Opposite page. Above, open-air buffet at Molsheim in 1910, on the occasion of the Prince Henry of Prussia Race. The young Ettore Bugatti is on the left: lanky and athletic, he already has the attentive, keen look which later distinguished him. Bottom, a drawing by Ettore Bugatti, published in the first catalogue, in 1910.

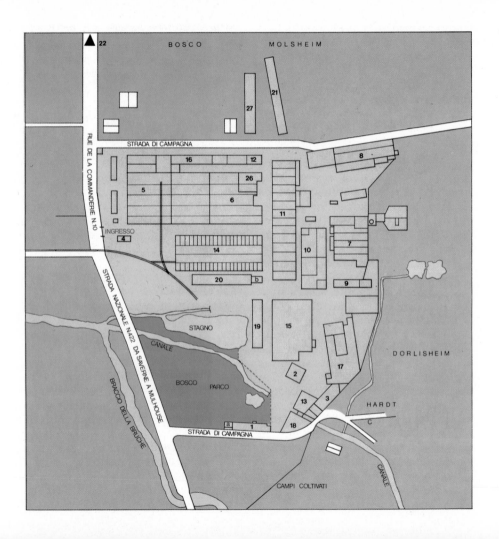

astonishing to realize that Bugatti in 1932 had conceived of and built the Type 53, a Grand Prix car with all-wheel drive. Bugatti's prolific creativity in the automotive sector was deeply linked to his activity as an inventor in other fields. Multi-faceted, relentless, egocentric: a genius. Outclassing such celebrated rivals as André Citroën, Louis Renault and especially the volcanic Gabriel Voisin, Bugatti was the greatest charismatic figure on the French motor-car scene until 1939, as well as sovereign over a microcosmic realm in the small Alsatian city of Molsheim, where he built his automobile factory, the family castle, stables for his beloved horses and a hotel-guesthouse for his customers ("L'Hostellerie du Pur-Sang"). He was sometimes arrogant but possessed a fervid, tumultuous mind. He designed railway auto-locomotives and powerboats, shoes with toe separation and fixed-head engines, remained faithful to the end to the rigid front axle but was the first to mount ribbon brakes on his rail-cars. He was a genius transcended by history and fate: the former unleashed a disastrous World War that sapped his energy, while the latter, on the very eve of that conflict, robbed him of his beloved son and designated heir, Jean, who perished in a motoring accident. He never recovered from the two catastrophes and, persecuted by those same French partisans who undermined

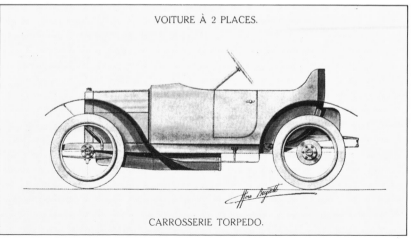

VOITURE À 2 PLACES.

CARROSSERIE TORPEDO.

Above. Molsheim, 1913. Ettore on horseback, next to a Type 15 with stage-coach body by Widerkher of Colmar. His two great loves: cars and horses. Centre. Gianni (Jean) Bugatti next to a Fiacre coupé with a Type 44 chassis. If he had not met a tragic death during night-time testing in 1939, he would have been the worthy inheritor of Ettore's work.

the health of Renault and Porsche, he died in 1947, sad and in dire financial straits, after remarrying and siring two more children, Thérèse and Michel.

He had just acquired French citizenship, in place of the Italian nationality he has always retained (though this did not prevent him from receiving the Légion d'Honneur in 1932). With his passing the Marque also sank into a wakeless slumber, and the surviving heirs (Ebé, Lidia and Roland) were unable (or unwilling?) to rouse it.

The "Bugatti Revival" is a recent phenomenon, following a couple of half-hearted attempts that had sought only to squeeze some profit out of the prestigious marque. And this rebirth came about thanks to the

efforts of one man, Romano Artioli. This modern-day revitalizer of the noble Marque was born in Mantua on 5 December 1932, but in 1937 his family moved to Bolzano, where the young Artioli with his brother began working in the car business, expanding his activities from an initial Opel dealership to the official Ferrari distributorship in Germany and the importation of Suzuki and Lotus in Italy, with his firm Autexpo which was based in Bolzano.

Now that he had become an entrepreneur with solid foundations, he decided to indulge the undying mechanical love he had nurtured since childhood: Bugatti. He confronted the challenging task of reviv-

Above. To excel, always and everywhere. This was Ettore Bugatti's creed. He won innumerable racing victories: this 1936 photograph taken at Montlhéry shows, from the left, William Grover-Williams, Pierre Weyron, Jean Bugatti and Jean Pierre Wimille.

9

ing the grand firm by taking a clean sheet of paper, assembling a core group of trusted, skilled people around him and earmarking a colossal investment plan for this undertaking that would give the new Bugatti all the substance and credibility such a marque deserved. The project was finalized around 1985, and naturally many shook their heads at the prospect of the pragmatic Tyrolian entrepreneur spending a fortune on such a dream. But work began vigorously on several fronts, with immediate solutions to a series of urgent problems. The company was formed on 1987 with the following management: Giampaolo Stanzani, formerly of Lamborghini (designer of the Countach), was engaged to design the mechanicals of the car, with bodystyling entrusted to Marcello Gandini. Architect Giampaolo Benedini was hired to design a completely new, original plant intended solely for construction of the future Bugatti and for possible future engineering work on contract. This plant was built at Campogalliano, not at Molsheim: the pragmatic Artioli was well aware that to create a small number of GTs with super specifications, he would need the expertise and experience of outside specialists already involved in these delicate processes, so the province of Modena obviously offered unbeatable potential. As time went by, Artioli's venture grew in size and daring,

and even the skeptics were forced to believe, when a big celebration at Campogalliano on 14 September 1990 showed industry observers how much had been accomplished to that point and confirmed the huge investments already made.

In the meantime, bitter contention between Artioli and Stanzani in the summer of 1990 had resulted in the latter's dismissal. His place was taken by Nicola Materazzi (ex-Ferrari) and by Pavel Rajmis (previously at Audi), while the prototypes of the new car had began to appear rather openly on the public roads. The rumors leaking from Campogalliano spoke of lofty technical specifications with staggering levels of performance, styling and pricing, befitting the Bugatti tradition. Then, during the summer of 1991, the final version of the new Bugatti was finally completed, tested and unveiled to the industry during a totally exceptional tour de force that began on 14 September 1991 at Paris, with a presentation at La Défense and dinner at Versailles, followed the next day by a party for Bugatti at Molsheim, then more presentations of the car and seminars on Bugatti at the Musée Nationale de l'Automobile at Mulhouse. Finally the car was unveiled to the Italian public at Campogalliano on 28 September 1991. Thus was born the new Bugatti, the car that deservingly sports that celebrated oval: the EB110.

Michel, Ettore's youngest son, next to the Type 57 belonging to Roland Wagner, chairman of the Fondation Bugatti. This car is of particular importance: a lantern in front of the radiator contains a small torch which was lit at Molsheim and taken to Campogalliano, the site of Bugatti's rebirth. This flame, "the symbol of a burning enthusiasm for Bugatti", was intended as a trait d'union between the old factory and the new one.

THE DESIGN

Reviving a venture of Bugatti caliber from scratch was clearly no simple matter. In fact, there was a moral obligation to affix this marque only on a car supreme enough to withstand inevitable comparisons to the former operation, and this was certainly not easy. It was not enough to build "only" a very good car: it had to be something truly exceptional, indisputable, an automobile with a Bugatti soul, in other words: only in this way could the new car earn the necessary respect.

Of course, this meant playing at the highest stakes, without compromises or dangerous self-patronage. It meant fearless confrontation with the absolute cream of ultra-sport motoring, with the best Ferraris and Lamborghinis, difficult competitors with excellent industrial and commercial organizations.

This face-off was also inevitable because of an historical fact: too often, in recalling the heroic Grand Prix racing era of the '30s, we remember the total dominance exerted in those races by the extraordinary Grand Prix Mercedes-Benz and Auto Unions from '35 to '39, and we note that Bugatti (as well as Alfa Romeo) was regularly crushed by the financial and organizational superiority of the great German teams. But we too often forget that this relationship was completely turned around when the term of comparison was road cars instead of sterile GP machines. In this sector, in many respects more indicative of the true capabilities of a carmaker, Alfa and Bugatti produced much better cars than their powerful Germanic rivals. For all its awesome appearance, and the terrifying shriek of its Kompressor, the Mercedes 540K was a very modest threat to the excellent performance of an Alfa 2900 or, even better, a Bugatti 57SC. A motorist seeking the utmost in fast road driving thus headed straight for Molsheim, not for Untertürkheim or Zwickau. The dazzling beauty of the fine carriage-work designed to attire the sophisticated chassis of the Patron clearly demonstrated the mechanical excellence of these extraordi-

A nearly definitive prototype version, photographed at Campogalliano. 13

nary cars, the true royalty of the road in those days. To put things into perspective, the "Tank" derived with few modifications from the 57 won the 24 Hours of Le Mans on a couple of occasions.

This is why recreating such a level of excellence was not a simple undertaking. Because of the enormous technological progress of recent years, constructing a new automobile has become an absolutely immense project, and its gestation re-quires years of work and copious funding, against gigantic risks. Romano Artioli was well aware of all this, and with his great experience in the super-GT sector he decided to even his odds by putting enormous personal and corporate re-sources into the project, initiating with a meticulous search for the "best at all costs" (people, first of all) and proceeding with almost fanatical care in each progressive stage of the operation.

14

Motorists driving along the Brenner Motorway near the Campogalliano exit in 1988 could observe the first tangible signs of the operation, when construction began on the original new plant with its magnificent design. A creation of architect Giampaolo Benedini, the plant is characterized by totally uncommon structural refinement for an industrial building. It became operational in 1991.

The block arrangement of the complex is interesting, because even figuratively it represents the diversified use of the individual blocks: the large crystal cylinder facing south, perhaps the most characterizing element in the complex, hosts the studies and research department; the central cube houses the management and offices; the large factory buildings set more to the north contain the actual production facilities. With its handsome design, the Bugatti plat at Campogalliano would certainly

15

have pleased the original Patron.

The car is equally radical. It, too, would have pleased the founder of the marque: perhaps he would have made it the same way himself, had he been active today. The car was christened the EB110, to celebrate the initials of the founder and the 110th anniversary of his birth at its official presentation in September 1991.

In determining the design content of a supercar with such a noble coat-of-arms, Romano Artioli set his sights from the outset on an ideal with no compromises, in which the maximum would be barely sufficient. The most advanced automotive technologies were therefore examined, evaluated and pondered. Surely the selection of the final configuration for the car must have been difficult, since the need to have the absolute maximum must have conditioned the entire process.

In the end, the design of the Bugatti EB110 shows that very few constraints were placed on the imagination of the designers in their thorough, sincere quest for technological innovation, not as an end unto itself but rather to the extent that it could enhance the car's performance, spirit or beauty to the highest level. Intelligently, in any case, this quest for technological supremacy was made secondary to one prevailing concept: designing a "human" supercar, not a Group C type monster unfit for road use but a real Gran

Turismo capable of dialoguing with the driver without any intimidation or fatigue or torture.

The result of this complex quest for the best possible interfacing between man and machine, plus the principle of top performance, was the EB110 design.

Giorgetto Giugiaro had his own views on modern Bugatti sports coupés, and unexpectedly presented this bodywork study at the April 1990 Turin Motor Show. It was judged to be interesting, but away from the Bugatti visual tradition.

17

THE BODY STYLING

Mechanical questions aside, the crux of reviving a marque as charged with forms and images as Bugatti would inevitably center around the question of styling. The importance Artioli and his team attributed to esthetics was evident from the inauguration of the factory, itself a successful example of high-level industrial design. Giampaolo Benedini, an architect in grand style, in fact, managed to shroud that plant with all the aura of the legend without compromising the practicality of a professional structure. Ettore Bugatti would undoubtedly have been pleased with it, especially with the almost obsessive repetition of his monogram throughout.

The car to be bodied had to respect some precise specifications, dictated by a desire to seek maximum performance (thus a two-seater, no luggage compartment, center-rear engine and ample space for mechanicals) and by a need to adapt this species of lines to the numerous standards regarding various aspects of the vehicle.

Without going into detail about all the compromises a designer must accept to get his creation homologated, it is clear that the need to place the headlamps a certain height from the road will condition the front end lines, while the air scoop dimensions may not exceed certain limits without being shielded by grilles (à la Testarossa). Even the stringent standards on emission and noise control force the stylist to reserve the necessary space for a highly developed exhaust system with catalytic converter.

Besides these strictly legal-bureaucratic demands, there is the more appealing technical side, which includes that all-important combination of good aerodynamic penetration (a key factor both for performance and noise abatement) together with sufficient downforce to prevent undesired handling problems at high speeds. A complex series of constraints, in other words. If we then add the fact that a grand GT of this level must offer its occupants good head- and leg-room, and that the driver must

The EB110 lifts its arms to the sky. Note the strong frontal, with the well-designed air vents.

have the best possible visibility of the surrounding world, we can appreciate what a complex task it was. It is no coincidence that the number of top-level supercar designers has been reduced to a handful: Giorgetto Giugiaro and Pininfarina in the lead, followed by the great tradition of Bertone, the talent of Greenley and then Wayne Cherry, author of the Calibra (we'd like to see what he could produce in this segment). Standing above them all is the undisputed Maestro, the man who since 1965 has continued to surprise the world with such breathtaking works as the Miura, Espada, Urraco, Countach, Stratos and Diablo: Marcello Gandini.

So in this search for the ultimate, the task of designing the EB110 was entrusted to this elegant Piedmontese gentleman. And he accomplished the job in record time, presenting a handsome sports coupé with somewhat boxy lines, which was approved and, with a few modifications, approved for production of the first prototypes. Then, however, the paths of Gandini and Artioli diverged and, in the search for a truly different bodystyle and one that was a product of the Campogalliano team, the job of designing the final bodywork was handed over to the Bugatti in-house Design Center, directed by Benedini. They set to work actively to give the future EB110 an even more personal look, adding to the constraints mentioned earlier a de-

sire to produce something unlike anything seen before. And they certainly succeeded.

The most characterizing feature of the EB110 is the front end, with a "face" that dominates the overall esthetics of the car. The esthetically strongest element of the old Bugattis, the horseshoe-shaped grille

Seen from the rear three-quarter view, the EB110 is immediately recognisable by the three lines of rectangular air inlets for engine cooling, the spoiler and the linear side panel.

with its proud vertical development, was eliminated for aerodynamic reasons, but a vestige of it was retained in the form of a small embellishment in the center of the massive front grillework, surmounted by the unmistakable oval trademark, with white lettering on a red background. The rounded form of the front end follows the modern tendency to optimize aerodynamic penetration: sharp creases on fenders, for example, always generate noisy, inefficient turbulence. In its visual impact, the spoiler/grille mass positioned below the headlights is efficient and offers good downforce.

Then there is another innovative detail

23

The rear spoiler is retractable. It automatically rises at speeds above 120 kph, and retracts when speed falls below 80 kph.

Rear overhead view. The cabin area is quite small compared to overall car size.

just above this, at the headlight level: the small headlamps with condenser (à la Opel Calibra) are, in fact, set inside a Plexiglas fairing, and this is both attractive and practical, since it eliminates the need to open the "eyelids" of the hideaway headlamp systems normally used on these supercars. What's more, this solution reduces the number of lighting elements present (the fixed accessory lamps for flashing are no longer needed), eliminating a heavy, archaic mechanism, and obviates the negative effect of the open "eyelid" on esthetics and aerodynamics.

The headlamp fairings are flanked by large air scoops, but the rest of the hood is

plain, as are the simple side-panels, with their high beltline, unbroken near the bottom by a neatly-inset air intake for the rear brakes and other viscera.

The doors open upward and forward, with the handles concealed in their lower edges (where the panel curves under to form the upper portion of the air scoops),

and just aft there are other small air intakes and the refueling ports.

The tail section is also simple, with a compact rear panel with venting louvers for the engine, closed above by a rear wing, which raises at high speeds but otherwise lies flush with the deck.

The windows of the car were designed

27

This page. The detailing design is clearly inspired by the figurative heritage of the old Bugattis.

Opposite page. EB110 side view. Note the considerable difference between front and rear overhangs.

29

both to allow acceptable interior dimensions and to offer good external visibility and low air resistance. Drag is further reduced by the flush mountings of the windshield and side windows. The side glasses lower completely inside the doors and have no frame molding: when the doors close, the windows slip into the weatherstripping for a perfect air and water seal. To permit this action, the glass is automatically lowered a few millimeters when the door handles are operated. The action is performed in reverse when the doors are closed, as in the BMW 850i, which has a similar device.

Important from the styling standpoint is the fact that the engine is completely visible under the vast rear window. With its perfect finish in every detail, this powerplant truly deserves to be on display. And then its low profile avoids any obstacle to rear visibility, while enclosing it would undoubtedly create problems of heat dissipation from the engine compartment, which must become a real Dante's Inferno during protracted use.

The wipers are the classic single-arm type without pantograph, with a smaller reinforcing blade and some special design features that improve adherence at high speeds. The same care displayed in the body fit and finish is echoed in the other external features, such as the magnificent light-alloy wheels produced by BBS ex-

Close up of the rear left light cluster.

clusively for Bugatti, with a totally original design. Also on the drawing-board is a new wheel with seven flat spokes to suggest the famous wheels of the Bugatti Type 35.

The interior was designed with particular care, since this is where automobiles of this breed show their pleasant side (as well as their rationality). The general layout of seats, dashboard, instrument cluster, main controls and accessories was kept classical, to avoid nagging inconveniences in driving the EB110. The instrumentation is particularly well-designed: clearly legible, clustered on a compact panel with analog dials easily visible between the steering wheel spokes.

And then there's wood: reminiscent of Bugatti's elegant grand routières, the EB100 is also embellished with burled walnut around the instruments and on the central panel. For those who disdain this foresty touch, however, there is an interesting alternative: the lightweight version (EB110 S) presented at the 1992 Geneva Motor Show eliminates the walnut to save on weight. This solution can also be requested on the "normal" version.

The EB110 is, therefore, a magnificent car. Very pretty, elegant and of gentle birth: one could wanting nothing more. It is very expensive of course, but quality and beauty have always been concepts which do not mix well with economy.

The radiator grille harks back to the original Bugattis, now legendary. Ettore Bugatti designed it, drawing his inspiration from a horseshoe.

The EB110 in front of the historic marque badge which dominates the wall of the factory at Campogalliano, designed by the architect Giampaolo Benedini.

Three more shots of the EB110 with the doors open. Many of today's super-cars have opted for this eye catch-ing kind of door opening. However, compared with the conventional kind, the mechanisms it requires are more complicated and delicate.

The EB110's cabin is functional and there are few concessions made to luxury, although there is some wooden trim. However, successive cars will be available with the choice of a Poltrona Frau interior.

The EB110 S was presented at the 1992 Geneva Motor Show. Called Versione Estrema (Extreme Version), the bodywork is lighter and the engine more powerful. The monochrome cabin is an interesting detail.

TECHNICAL DESCRIPTION

The Bugatti EB110 is a two-seat berlinetta, or sports coupé, with center-rear-mounted longitudinal supercharged engine, carbon-fiber frame and permanent all-wheel drive. This scheme suggests that, apart from the many refinements used in dressing the EB110, it is the mechanical side that best reflects the enormous engineering efforts of the Campogalliano firm. In fact, everything that lies beneath the elegant Bleu France of the bodywork is so radical and extreme that it somewhat transcends comparison with best traditional supercars. The Bugatti EB110, in other words, is in many respects a breed apart. A significant contribution toward this result was provided by the technical sponsors: Elf, Aérospatiale, Michelin and Messier-Hispano-Bugatti placed all their technology at the disposal of the Italian firm in the form of specially-designed systems of unlimited excellence. The same is true of the other suppliers outside this pool: BBS for wheels, Brembo for brakes, ZF for steering and synchronizers, Diavia for the climate-control system, IHI for the turbo-compressors and Nakamichi for the car stereo system.

The EB110 seems an ideal response to those enthusiasts who for years have been praising the excellence of the Ferrari F40's engine and the chassis (with drive systems) of the Porsche 959, because it manages to offer a highly convincing amalgamation of state-of-the-art technology in the various assemblies under a single body shell.

The primary focal point of such a high-performance car is, of course, the engine. This one is a 60° V-12, all light-alloy, with 81 mm of bore, 56.6 mm of stroke, a compression ratio of 7.5:1 and piston displacement of 3499.92 cc. The overall layout of the engine is relatively classic, but the twin-cam timing system controls 60 valves, five per cylinder (36 intake and 24 exhaust). Other refinements include gear drive on the timing system, special pistons (Borgo or Mahle), a multipoint electronic fuel-injection system designed and built

The EB110's powerful engine: a 60°V 3.5-litre 12 cylinder, with four turbos. It develops maximum output of 550 HP, and is one of the prettiest engines ever built for a road car.

41

by Bugatti, ignition with a single coil per cylinder and titanium con-rods produced by Panki. The relatively limited displacement does not jeopardize power: thanks to its four turbo-compressors, this engine cranks out an average 550 bhp at 8,500 rpm. The use of small-diameter turbines helps enhance the torque curve, as demonstrated by the strong 62 mkg furnished at 3,500. Obviously, the specific power of this engine is exceptional: an impressive 157.2 bhp/liter. The formidable performance of this power unit, with the resulting high temperatures and flow rates, led to the development of a special oil by Elf, based on the best available technology, called "Competition Bio". The lubrication system has a dry sump design, partly in an effort to reduce the vertical dimension of the engine, which is positioned, as we said, longitudinally behind the driver to optimize weight distribution. The final drive gear is in the front end of the engine, where we find the dry single-disc clutch with hydraulic servo-assist. From here the torque enters the gearbox and is distributed to the three differentials. Even the positioning of the clutch is highly original, since it is also longitudinal, sitting parallel to and alongside the crankshaft (its housing is part of the crankcase). This helps lower the center of gravity and reduce longitudinal dimensions (the wheelbase is only 2,550 mm) and explains the

slightly off-center position of the EB110's engine. Although the gearbox housing is cast into the crankcase, its lubrication system is separate from the engine's, since the two require different oils. The transmission is a six-speed with ZF synchronizers plus reverse (unsynchronized). The powerplant is liquid-cooled, of course, while the exhaust system has an excellent three-way catalytic converter. Special attention was devoted to reducing engine noise, and the results are truly among the best in its class. The self-locking rear differential receives 72% of the power. The remaining 28% is sent to the self-locking central unit and then relayed on to the front differential via a superb carbon-fiber driveshaft. The all-wheel drive is permanent.

To obtain the best possible combination of lightness and rigidity, the frame is made of carbon fiber by Aérospatiale, which has a dozen years of experience in using this material, ensuring maximum quality and durability. The frame incorporates the mount-points for the principal assemblies. The suspensions repeat the time-tested pattern of the best GTs, with upper and lower A-arms, telescoping dampers (double in the rear), helical springs and anti-roll bars. Their geometry was studied to permit the use of ABS, and they offer an exceptionally long vertical wheel travel, ensuring outstanding roadholding characteristics with no loss in riding comfort. This

The car is rear-engined. Even the oil sump is painted the bleu France of the old Bugattis.

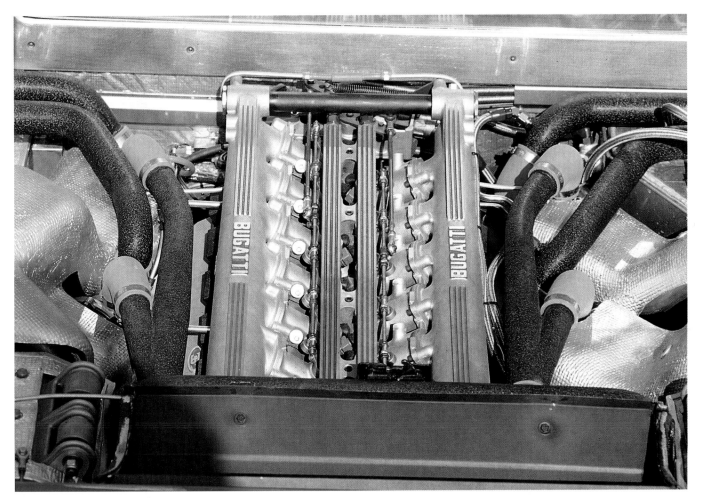

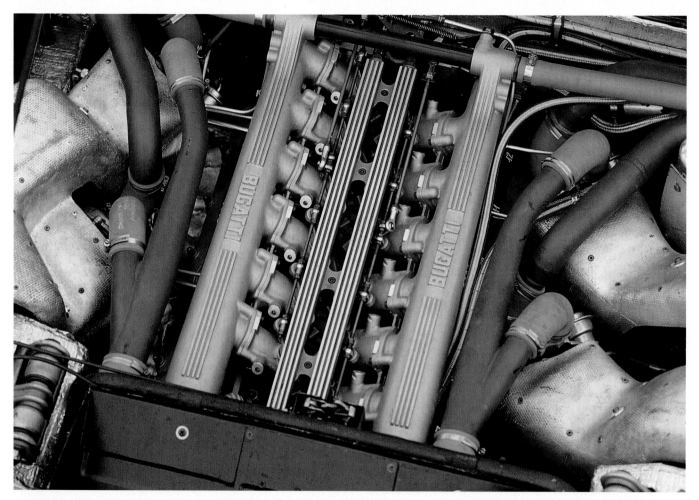

classic configuration will be mounted on the early units produced, while a hydro-pneumatic circuit developed by Messier-Hispano-Bugatti will be offered on later production. In this system, precharged gas will replace the springs, while fluid will provide the damping action. Since testing on this system is already at an advanced stage, it should be ready for delivery right after the first few units. As we shall see further on, however, not even the initial purchasers will have to relinquish the benefits of the advanced MHB system.

The brakes, supplied by Brembo, are state-of-the-art, of course. Oversized, self-vented discs (330 x 32 mm) are used to permit better heat dissipation through the venting outlets, and the units are servo-assisted and ABS-controlled, a "must" feature on such a supercar. The light-alloy wheels produced by the specialists at BBS measure 9x18" in front and 12x18" in the rear and mount Michelin MXX3 tires of 245/40-18" and 325/30-18", respectively.

A careful ergonomic study was conducted on the cockpit, to optimize the driveability of the EB110 under all conditions. Despite the car's low profile (1,115 mm), this was accomplished thanks to the generous glass area, the rational arrangement of primary and secondary controls, the tidy layout of the dashboard and analog instrumentation and the overall simplicity of the interior, purposely designed in this man-ner to avoid distracting the driver with nonessential gadgetry. But this naturally detracts in no way from the luxury and fine craftsmanship of the passenger compartment. The strong point of the EB110 is that the enormous engineering effort expended on it has produced an automobile that offers driving pleasure greater than many competitive models while alleviating (and in most cases eliminating) many of the discomforts and inconveniences previously deemed standard equipment on this category of supercars. One example of the success of this approach is the effort focused on one traditional weakness of the grand Italian-style supercars: the climate control system. For the EB110, in fact, Diavia engineered a totally new system that offers constant, efficient temperature and humidity control even under extreme conditions. Since poor climate control can also cause significant functional problems (fogged windows, for example, can dangerously reduce visibility), obtaining good performance in this area should not be considered just a luxury but a true necessity, and an aid to safe driving. On the subject of comfort, the absence of a conventional luggage compartment, since all the space under the bodywork is occupied by mechanical assemblies and sundry systems, is partially offset by the possibility of stowing a specially designed bag behind the seats.

The EB110's engine is the first road-car engine with 5-valve per cylinder timing.

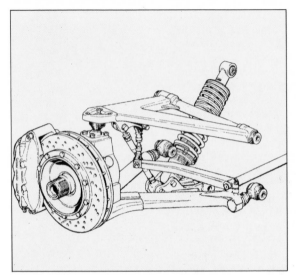

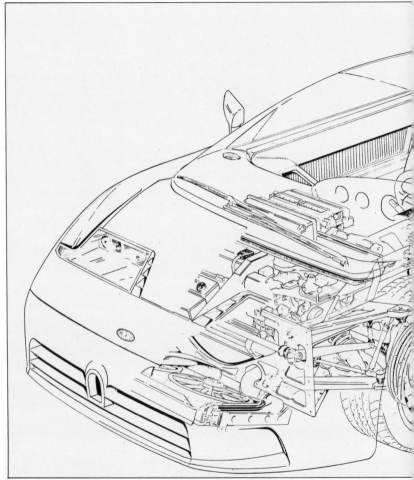

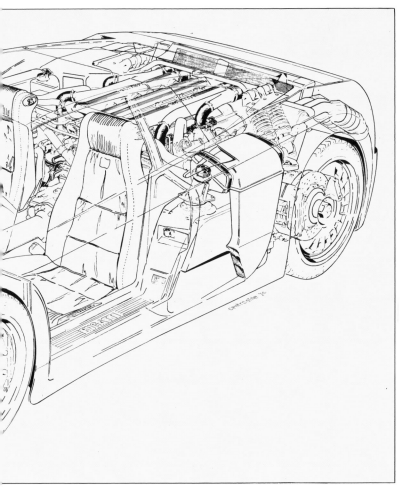

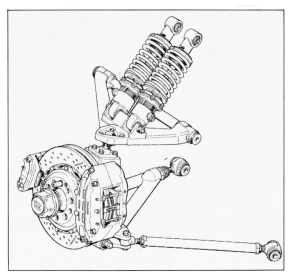

X-ray of the whole of the EB110. At the sides, the front and rear suspensions.

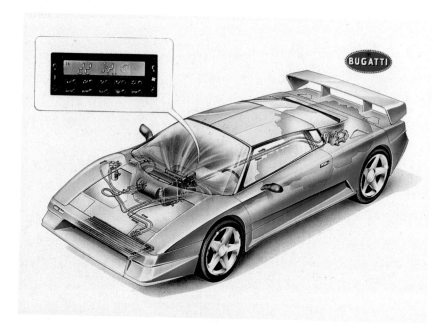

Tangible proof of Bugatti's awareness that playing a front-line role in technical production advancement need not result in unequal customer treatment is the company policy on the distribution of its cars. Production, limited to 200 units per year, will be dedicated to enthusiasts who can demonstrate they possess the necessary requisites to "deserve" an EB110. The cars will therefore be assigned only to persons judged worthy by a special commission, and the traditional plate bearing the chassis number will also indicate the name of the car's original owner. This assignment will be rigorously controlled, so for this reason Bugatti Automobili will have no external dealerships, at least initially. The EB110 can thus be acquired only directly from the manufacturer, with no true list price established. The first cars delivered (May 1992) have "conventional" suspensions, but Bugatti has undertaken to offer a five-year full guarantee on the EB110, including automatic retrofitting of the cars whenever new technical refinements are introduced. So any customer so desiring may ask to have his car retrofitted with the MHB hydro-pneumatic system with no difficulty.

In completing the technical description of this extraordinary supercar, we should not disregard certain industrial aspects of the company which, rather than depart from the spirit of the EB110, actually under-

Diagram visualising the heating and ventilation flows of the Diavia climate control system.

score the seriousness of the firm's intentions with a unique example of devotion in this field. The Campogalliano plant, for example, is not merely a production center. Apart from its superb architecture, it is enhanced by a total devotion to the marque, demonstrated by an imposing work of documentation (under the guidance of scholar Ivo Ceci) with which the company intends to develop research on the long and complex history of Bugatti through the creation of a large, well-organized documentary archive. This work of intelligent scholarship is even better expressed through the construction of the magnificent Ora Cultural Center, in which the activity of Bugatti rises to the level of a cult and which, with its inimitable blend of futurism and culture, is the only sanctuary of its kind in automotive history. The Bugatti plant includes innovative architectural solutions particularly regarding the services, which would be too numerous to list here. It is more interesting to know that the 90,000 sq.meters of land occupied by the current complex is being expanded and that within its confines, amid spacious, manicured lawns, there is a heliport and a test track. And a new test layout is currently under construction that will permit higher speeds in total safety, on an additional 80,000-sq.m lot recently acquired adjacent to the plant. The new annex will also include more laboratory facilities.

The Bugatti site at Campogalliano, in the province of Modena. Emilia was preferred to Alsace because of the skilled workforce.

49

Prototypes in various stages of preparation at Campogalliano. A hand-built process is used, to ensure the level of quality which is essential for such a noble marque.

The factory equipment is absolutely state-of-the-art. Special attention was devoted to the study of the work areas, with perfect ergonomics throughout. Naturally, no effort was spared in this search for perfection, in either financial or human terms. All this has an impact not only on the EB110's desirability as a supercar of supreme level but also on the credentials of Bugatti Automobili as a producer of know-how on contract. The engineering activity of the Campogalliano firm is developing rapidly, in fact, qualifying this company as one of the future driving forces in the automotive industry. This is one reason why, just when a relative crisis in the industry has been forcing surrounding plants to scale back their projects and ambitions, Bugatti has continued to hire highly qualified personnel, reaching the respectable staffing level of 160 (March '92). This significant employment level is also symbolic of the enthusiasm and confidence in the future of the company management, first of all Romano Artioli, flanked by a team of top specialists recruited for their impeccable credentials in the supercar segment. The EB110 design, in fact, is credited to three engineers extremely well-known in this field: Oliviero Pedrazzi, Tiziano Benedetti and Achille Bevini. Nicola Materazzi, an engineer whose background includes work on the Lancia Stratos, the Osella F1 and various Ferrari road-cars, including the F40, is in charge of the technical department. Stefano Mion (former Lamborghini engineer) is production manager. Czech-born Pavel Rajmis, trained at Tatra and Audi, runs the test department, while Jean-Philippe Vittecoq is lead test-driver and thus responsible for vehicle testing.

A final note inevitably concerns the corporate structure of an operation that, precisely because of its lofty level, could only be managed through a sophisticated financial structure. At the top of the pyramid stands Bugatti International S.A.H. (headquarters in Luxembourg, chairman J.M. Borel), which controls 70% of Ettore Bugatti S.r.l., with head offices at Ora (Bolzano), chaired by R. Kettmeier, created to safeguard the trademark and services. It owns 100% of Bugatti International Gestion (Luxembourg), which controls licenses, royalties, etc. It also controls 80% of Bugatti Automobili S.p.A. of Campogalliano, with Romano Artioli as chairman. The remaining 20% of this last firm is owned by FI.SI.CO. (financial strongbox of the Artioli family, which holds 18%) and some technical shareholders (2%). This complex corporate structure, designed for a better division of tasks and responsibilities, actually makes the various expressions of this "Bugatti Revival" more agile in interacting with the numerous outside organizations.

The composite honeycomb chassis, in carbonfibre and Nomex, weighs 125 kg. It was produced by the French firm Aérospatiale, traditionally in the forefront of composite constructions. 51

EB110

ENGINE
Disposition: longitudinally-mounted mid-engine
Materials: aluminium and titanium
Cylinders: 12 in V 60°
Bore and stroke: 81x56.6 mm (3.18x2.22 in)
Piston displacement: 3499 cc (213.6 cu in)
Compression ratio: 7.5:1
Maximum power: 405 kW (550 HP) at 8000 rpm
Maximum torque: 590 Nm (60 kgm) at 3800 rpm
Timing system: DOHC, 5 valves per cylinder
Fuel feed: Bugatti multipoint fuel injection, 4 IHI
turbochargers
Lubrication: forced-feed
Cooling system: cooling liquid, forced-feed
Emission control system: 4 3-way catalyzers and heated Lambda sonde

DRIVELINE
Drive: permanent 4-wheel drive, torque distribution
front 27%, rear 73%
Clutch: dry single-plate
Gearbox: 6-speed + Rev mechanic
Gear ratios: 1st = 3.757, 2nd = 2.521, 3rd = 1.834, 4th =
1.424 5th = 1.148, 6th = 0.949, Rev = 4.252
Final ratio: front 3.090, central 2.704, rear 3.182

Differential: free front differential, central viscous coupling, rear self-blocking

CAR BODY
Type: 2-door, 2-seater sports coupé
Frame: single-block in carbon fibre
Front suspension: independent wheels with keystone
wishbone, pull-rod system
Rear suspension: independent wheels with keystone
wishbone
Steering system: rack and pinion, power-assisted,
Ø 12 m
Brakes: ventilated discs (Ø 332 mm), power-assisted,
Bosch/Bugatti ABS system
Rims: front 9" x 18", rear 12" x 18"
Tyres: front 245/40 R18X9J, rear 325/30 R18X12J
Fuel tank: 120 l (26.5 imp.gal.)

DIMENSIONS AND WEIGHTS
Length: 4400 mm (173.2 in)
Width: 1960 mm (77.1 in)
Height: 1125 mm (44.4 in)
Wheelbase: 2550 mm (100.3 in)
Front and rear tracks: 1550/1618 mm (61/63.7 in)
Kerb weight: 1618 kg (3595 lbs)

PERFORMANCES
Top speed: 340 kph (212 mph)
Acceleration from 0 to 100 kph: 3.6 sec
1 km from standing start: 19.9 sec
Speed per 1000 rpm (5th gear): 40 kph
Consumption at 90/120/urban cycle: 9/13/21 l/100 km
Specific power: 157.7 HP/liter (2.57 HP/cu in)
Weight to power ratio: 2.67 kg/HP (6.53 lbs/HP)

EB110S

EB110 specifications except:

ENGINE
Maximum power: 442 kW (600 HP) at 8000 rpm
Maximum torque: 610 Nm (62 kgm) at 3600 rpm

DIMENSIONS AND WEIGHTS
Kerb weight: 1418 kg (3151 lbs)

PERFORMANCES
Maximum speed: 350 kph (218 mph)
Acceleration from 0 to 100 kph: 3.4 sec
1 km from standing start: 18.8 sec
Consumptions 90/120/urban c.: 8.5/13/19 l/100 km
Specific power: 171.4 HP/l (2.84 HP/cu in)
Weight to power ratio: 2.36 kg/HP (5.25 lbs/HP)

The power and torque curve of the Bugatti EB110.

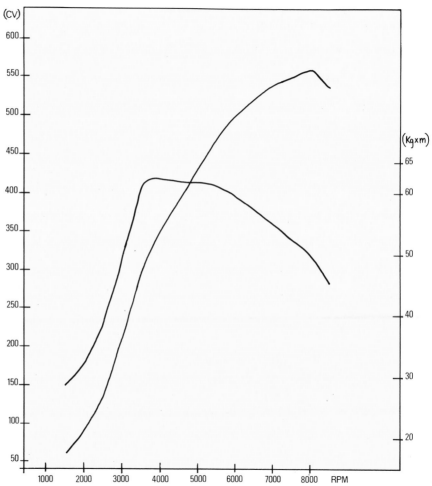

53

THE PRESENTATION OF THE EB 110

from "Le Grandi Automobili" no. 37. Fall, 1991.

A recent survivor of Frankfurt and its blinding Motor Show, it was worthwhile hopping the first plane and heading for Paris. September 14th 1991 was the date planned for the presentation of the new Bugatti, another rebirth of a myth which has become oxydised in the post-war years and which an entrepreneur with an enormous heart (and a wallet probably of similar proportions), Romano Artioli, has caused to rise again. The presentation of the magnificent plant in which the new car has been designed and is to be built took place a year before, on 14th September 1990, thus celebrating the 109th year since the birth of Ettore Bugatti. It goes without saying that exactly one year later was the right time to make up one of the round numbers so suited to creating a high class badge. Here, therefore, is the EB 110: the Patron's years and his initials. Pefect.

In view of the eminently French nature of the Bugatti epopea, it was quite natural that the new car's presentation should take place in Paris, heart, brain and metallic belly of the Hexagon. So it was that there was also an opportunity to content the female sex, in whom the very idea of this city causes uncontrollable and inconceivable hormonal upsets: it must also be admitted that a warm, sunlit and windless September such as the one which framed the weekend of the "Bugatti Awakening" is decidedly pleasing, renders this city more beautiful and helps one to survive the main attractions (the Gare d'Orsay, Hermès in the Faubourg St. Honoré, the Centre International de l'Automobile at Pantin etc.). At 11 o'clock the morning after, I was at the Parvis de la Défense, nose in the air and mouth open to gaze at the majestic Arc, the dark glass Fiat bricks, Elf's splendid asymetrical tower. The big square was filled with castor oil vapours and musical growls: fifty or so old Bugattis from all over Europe were spread out in rays around a kind of small, domed tent, in Bleu France, under which was the so long awaited EB 110.

The longed-for press conference was at

The EB 110 still covered by a tarpaulin, which only allows its proportions to be revealed. Above, the invitation to attend the EB 110's presentation at Campogalliano.

55

Opposite page. Many well-known faces were present at the presentation, from the automotive world and not. But the glorious ancestors could certainly not be left out, and were present to underline the continuity of an automotive philosophy which, notwithstanding a long interruption, has never died. Above, the invitation to attend the EB110's international presentation in Paris.

12 o'clock, inside the Elf skyscraper and included an interesting assortment of speakers: Romano Artioli in the foreground, then an alluringly aged Alain Delon, the extremely elegant chairman of Elf with a suit worthy of Cary Grant at his best, with glasses à la Professor Jones (Indiana), Materazzi who is an ex Ferrari engineer with a great reputation whose considerable burden will be to put the EB110 into production, the architect Benedini, the test-driver Vittecoq and the czechoslovak engineer Rajmis.

Strangely, but then perhaps not, the event had not attracted many specialists from the rarified world of the super GTs. There were certainly some illustrious absences at the press conference, and those present passed a rather sterile hour with a few questions to which Artioli replied with his customary politeness, helped by Delon. From such questions and answers it was possible to draw the conclusion that Gandini and Stanzani have been burnt in effigy at Campogalliano, that the "Modenese" option (instead of a resurrection at Molsheim, let there be no misunderstanding) was rendered obligatory by the territory and the labour force available there. After which, without having ascertained who owns Luxemburg based "Bugatti International" who are financing a conspicuous 80% of the project, who is really the firm's current technical director

and what length of time is predicted for world-wide homologation, the price and other pleasantries of the sort (but refreshed by the idea that anyone who wants to buy an EB 110 will have to deal directly with Artioli and submit themselves to the judgement of a kind of college of arbiters in order to be considered, at the end, deserving of buying one...), we finally all went out into the increasingly scorching Parisian sun for lunch, which was care of the very Flo. It was therefore, quite frankly exceptional, with wonderful examples of every God given thing, and with great wines which were luckily well-chilled. This helped overall survival whilst awaiting the Event, and the well-being of the VIPs present, two of whom - Ferruccio Lamborghini and Mauro Forghieri - produced clear evidence of how empathies between bordering factories can be serenely cultivated.

The lines of the EB 110 were certainly quite clean, but its unusual proportions were disconcerting, as was a nose decidedly more important that the miniscule tail, and a definite air of overall compactness masking dimensions which are exactly halfway between the Ferrari F40 and the Lamborghini Diablo. No doubt it is not easy for those who have to create something which is an heir to the sensational Atalante, Atlantique, Stelvio and Aérolithe, to overcome the mysterious

The EB110 surrounded by admirers in the middle of the Défense.

barricades which stand between imitation and innovation, the pedestrian and the sublime, scandal and emotion, but from such a long gestation period one expected something more amazing. Because apart from anything else, the awesome mechanicals, which are exactly what Stanzani showed me immediately after their assembly at Campogalliano in April 1990, is enough to make competitors' wrists shake: light alloy, 3.5-litre V12 engine, DOHC, 5-valves per cylinder, four intercooled turbos with electronic injection by an integrated engine management system, producing 550 HP at 8000 rpm, conrods and other metalwork in titanium, joints and

pipework up to aerospatial spec., 6-speed lenghtways gearbox cast parallel to the in-bloc engine. All-round traction with viscous coupling and carbonfibre transmission, power split prevalently to the back (27% to the front against 73% to the rear), carbonfibre chassis, etc. etc. To sum up, superb mechanicals designed and built in the most Pharaonic breadth of means and approach.

At the end of the presentation at the Défense, after the EB110 had fled with a curious over-muffled growl in the direction of Place de la Concorde, we all set off in a rush to change into DJs and evening dresses, to leave with the 7 o'clock coach

Following this the EB110 was transferred to its most congenial habitat: the Musée National de l'Automobile in Mulhouse, which previously housed the amazing Schlumpf collection. Note the "belle époque" lamps, identical to the ones on the Alexandre I bridge over the Seine in Paris.

Romano Artioli, project leader and boss of the reborn Bugatti.

from the Ritz in Place Vendôme for Versailles. And punctually at 19.00 hours we were on a bus crammed to the roof with evening *toilettes*. We arrived at 8.20 in one of the palace car parks beautified by a series of old Bugattis and a varied assortment of supercars, including a Giugiaro Nazca, and at last we were able to relax in the legendary gardens with music by Haendel and Vivaldi (which sounded curiously incongrous as background music to the waterworks of the French fountains). And at the crucial moment we finally went into the stupendous Orangerie, an extraordinary place with the dimensions and the cleansed rigorousness of an underground cathedral of five centuries ago. Stupendous, and the sight of the 170 tables each set for 10, sumptuously laid in this incredible scenario decidedly made one forget the actual car... just as well, since the EB 110 was not there. That's right, the queen of the show, the creature around which the entire event rotated, had not even been taken to Versailles, leaving the guests with their noses pressed against the window. Perhaps it was already on its way, together with the other more angled (but alluring) pre-production "mules", towards Molsheim, for the presentation the next day in the Alsatian town which was the birthplace of the Bugatti legend.

The scenario however was worthy of Hollywood; wisely choosing a table on the outside of the room in order to appreciate the extent of this room and the organisation responsible for serving the 1700 seated guests at the same time, thanks to the simultaneous comings and goings of 170 waiters in Indian file with relative dishes and/or bottles. A considerable show.

The continuation of the Versailles dinner, deprived of the catalytic presence of the EB 110, was very pleasant, but rather surrealistically detached from automotive subjects, to the joy of the wives and I believe of many other VIPs who were doubtless fed up with pistons and turbines. The food and the wine were good, it was a truly luxurious and successful evening.

The day after, having spent a day walking around a half-deserted Paris, there was the final surprise: on the bulging Paris-Bologna flight I embarked together with the troops from Campogalliano, who had been to see "their" car's first night. Well it was like being at Sant'Agata three years ago: a lengthy series of well-known and familiar faces, fugitives from Ferrari and Lamborghini, all together under a new trademark and in a new adventure. Modena, Modena....

Alain Delon, a legend and a connoisseur of the Bugatti marque, presents the EB110.

DRIVING IMPRESSIONS

All the technical prerequisites are here. And this new extreme supercar bears a trademark that alone is sufficient to quicken the pulse of aficionados. Its bodylines are also appealing and powerful, and its fine Bleu France hue is reminiscent of a string of racing victories with few equals in motor-sports history.

Bugatti: a red oval on a nose that no longer possesses the proud vertical structure of the radiators of yore. It now stands almost horizontal on a smooth, efficient, tidy, solid surface.

Can such a modern car be a true Bugatti? Sure, the devotion of Artioli's disciples in this undertaking leaves little room for doubt. The EB110 has a look that transmits a real, uncontaminated passion for the marque that transcends mere financial interests. Perhaps it's just an impression, but under its sleek sheet-metal we perceive not the enormous sum invested in the operation but rather an act of love by one who has wagered a sizable portion of his professional life in this endeavor. This pleasant impression, wholly worthy of the Bugatti mystique, is underscored by the visible satisfaction of the person who delivers the first definitive EB100 for our road test. The pride of marque that typifies all those who work in the grand GT factories scattered across the Modena area here reaches an almost metaphysical height, above the materiality of the object, as though everyone here at Campogalliano were aware of the impelling need to sustain his part in a noble, long-overdue mechanical Crusade.

We can't help but admire such involvement, suggestive of the charisma of the Bugatti trademark. Such impressions inevitably pervade anyone approaching such an automobile, especially if he has been a member of the Bugatti Owners' Club for over a decade.

In a more technical vein, the EB110 from the outside has the classic look of the super-sporty berlinettas, those that require the physical characteristics of an Alain Prost to fit comfortably inside, or at

The EB110's unapproachable performance figures are its most riveting feature: 340 kph and 3.6 seconds to 100 kph. No production car anywhere in the world can match it.

63

least the agility of a Bulgarian gymnast to climb in without scraping of the extremities. So the first surprise comes when we open the door up and forward (the handle concealed on its lower edge) and find that access is easy and the interior generously roomy. In fact, once positioned in the excellent driver's seat, we can appreciate the intelligence of a cockpit where we can sit comfortably, with total visual command of the outside world through the abundant glass area, ensconced in truly pleasant, luxurious surroundings.

The main and secondary controls are wisely positioned, and the very simplicity of the instrumentation indicates how much effort was expended to make this car "human" and driver-friendly. Even the clear view of the car's four corners (an apparently pedantic observation, but an attribute absolutely critical in normal city driving) is certainly better than usual. Despite some affection for the unrefined character of Italian GTs, we can't help applauding the intelligent overall design for offering these conveniences.

The engine starts instantly. The idle is immediately stable and regular, despite the myriad devices concealed in the engine compartment, and the noise is minimized by the well-designed exhaust system and the four turbo-compressors, silent in their own right.

It is always good manners to allow the

engine a few minutes to reach a reasonable temperature before setting out. So when the water temp indicator leaves the bottom of its scale, we can move off, and here other pleasant surprises are in the offing. The clutch, in fact, is extremely smooth and easy to handle, nothing like the stiff pedals we are used to finding on other 12-cylinders from this neighborhood. Even shifting into first (after all, the gearbox fluid is still cold, let's remember) is easy, linear, requiring no excessive flexing of the right arm muscles. The same is true of the superb power steering, and the combined facility of these controls lets the EB110 move onto the road with the same virile suppleness as a Porsche Carrera 4.

The gratification of the EB110 does not all derive from these friendly controls, however.

The engine is mellow and smooth-running, and the fact that torque reaches its peak at only 3500 rpm makes frequent gear-shifting unnecessary, even on this six-speed unit. In such a well-designed environment, where interior noise is minimized and driving comfort frankly unexpected for a supercar with such performance figures, accelerating is a natural reaction. And when we begin cornering at greater speeds, we realize the two dominant characteristics of the EB110's chassis. The first is that cornering is a precise operation in this car, thanks to its excellent

Seen on the move from on high, the EB110 changes from a static sculpture to a powerful mile-eating vector.

Over 4000 rpm engine response, already exceptional up to this speed, becomes overwhelming. What is more, the four-wheel drive nails every ounce of horsepower to the ground, avoiding the sliding around which is a common occurrence with rear-drive supercars.

steering qualities and the carefully designed suspensions. The other is that there is very little roll, despite the long vertical wheel travel.

As the engine warms, we become better acquainted with this extraordinary super-GT: this is the moment to start pushing it more meaningfully. While acceleration up to 4000 rpm is fine for general-purpose driving, the triggering of the four turbos above that level transfigures the "civil" impression we have had of the Bugatti thus far. This docile masterpiece of engineering is transformed into a powerful thoroughbred that surges forward with a throaty, multi-tone roar, harmonizing with the whistle of its countless gears and the ferocious whine of its turbines, all blended with the deep, velvety rumble of its exhausts. It is an extremely exciting sound, powerful but never offensive or excessive, wholly worthy of the wonderful machinery that produces it and an apt sound-track to the "Bugatti revival".

The acceleration pushes us well back into the fine leather seatback, and what are more than reasonable safety distances for any other car suddenly become alarmingly short as the Bugatti catapults ahead. The classic 0-100 km/h acceleration test is even more dramatic in some respects. Although the weight-power ratio of the EB110 is not much greater than that of some of its excellent rivals, what makes the difference is the

exceptional quality of its four-wheel drive. Thanks to this feature, it is not necessary to feather the throttle delicately to avoid power-dispersive slippage of the drive wheels. Here you flatten the accelerator against the floorboard, pop off the clutch (provided you have the heart to inflict such mistreatment on such a fine car, of course) and the Bugatti simply leaps forward, its big Michelins angrily biting into the asphalt with no intention of yielding. Under these conditions, the 3.7 seconds declared by the manufacturer are perfectly realistic, and clocking it is not so difficult, even though we aren't in the Ayrton Senna class.

Unleashing most of its 550 horses, the Bugatti quickly reaches its upper speed range, where highly functional brakes are a must. Here again, nothing is left to chance, as the mighty Brembo system offers effective braking power, with the watchful assistance of the ABS. This is particularly useful on slippery road surfaces, where the outstanding traction properties of the EB110 are truly in their element. And when we push the speed toward the upper limits, the carbon-fiber frame remains incredibly rigid, allowing the front and rear suspensions to show their stuff, with constant grip over any type of surface. And this tenacity seems to increase as the speed rises.

The EB110 handles with perfect neutrality up to a certain level of lateral acceleration, beyond which we begin to feel a slight tendency to understeer, quite easy to control. Directional stability is really exceptional even at high speed, the product of a wise split of power between the two axles and the painstaking aerodynamic design.

To help create proper downforce on the rear wheels, a rear wing has been incorporated into the bodywork: invisible up to 120 km/h, it is raised up when that speed is exceeded and returns to its hidden position when the speedometer drops below 80 km/h.

Due in part to this stability, driving the EB110 is truly pleasurable and doesn't drain the driver's energy, as occurs with many traditional sports coupés. The dialogue with this Bugatti is so benign that one experiences the 1990s equivalent of the joy of driving a 55 or a 57SC. And that's an accomplishment.

With the EB110, Bugatti Automobili has been victorious in several respects. From the technical standpoint, it has created from scratch a extraordinarily gifted car valid from every angle, a berlinetta that represents true progress for the reknowned school of super-sports coupés to which it belongs. From the ethical-psychological standpoint, perhaps the riskiest aspect to confront because of the many complex implications of such a prestigious marque, it has avoided all the land mines

With the performance in mind, safety was uppermost. Everything has been excellently seen to: the brakes are effective and the structure has a high degree of rigidity.

with which the history of similar "revivals" is strewn.

The company which has been so patiently and lovingly constructed at Campogalliano and Ora now stands as a monument to integrity. In this sense the EB110 is much more than a simple, though stupefying, automobile. It is the symbol of top-level savoir faire that will certainly glorify the French colors it bears and the technical sponsors who helped make the whole thing possible. But it is also confirmation that for many reasons the most splendid wheeled Phoenixes can only be resurrected in Italy. Well-deserved congratulations to Romano Artioli. Without people of his ilk, Italy would be a much more arid place to live and work.

Naturally-appearing phenomena in high-performance cars, such as understeer and roll, only occur when the car is driven in limit conditions. The overall stability is extraordinary.

70

*Automobilia wishes to thank Bugatti Automobili at
Campogalliano and its Chairman, Romano Artioli,
for the supply of material and for providing a car
for the road-test.*